BADCATS

Pat Thomson

OXFORD
UNIVERSITY PRESS

Great Clarendon Street, Oxford, OX2 6DP,
United Kingdom

Oxford University Press is a department of the University of Oxford.
It furthers the University's objective of excellence in research, scholarship,
and education by publishing worldwide. Oxford is a registered trade mark of
Oxford University Press in the UK and in certain other countries

Text © Pat Thomson 2003

The moral rights of the author have been asserted

First published in this edition 2016

British Library Cataloguing in Publication Data
Data available

978-0-19-837719-1

3 5 7 9 10 8 6 4 2

Paper used in the production of this book is a natural, recyclable product
made from wood grown in sustainable forests. The manufacturing process
conforms to the environmental regulations of the country of origin.

Printed in China by Leo Paper Products Ltd.

Acknowledgements
Cover and inside illustrations by Mike Phillips
Inside cover notes written by Sasha Morton

Contents

Chapter 1
In the Shed

Don't ever walk down Wall Street after dark.

If you do, don't go to Number 27.

If you do, at least stay away from the garden shed.

Why? Because things happen there. After dark, the Badcat Gang meet in the shed. You don't want to meet The Big Paw.

No, you really don't.

One moonlit night, at midnight,
a black cat slipped through the open
shed door.

That was Dodger.

Sharp enough to grab the best things
to eat. Fast enough to be out through the
window before anyone can catch him. He's
the best thief in the gang.

A bigger, grey cat padded down
the path. His eyes winked green in the
moonlight. One of his ears was torn. He
walked lightly but his muscles rippled
under thick, grey fur.

He turned his head. For a moment,
he showed his sharp teeth. Then
he, too, slipped into the shed.

That was Scrapper. He is fierce. He is
strong. What he loves best is a fight.

A much smaller cat dropped out of
the apple tree. As she crossed the
moonpath, her white front showed
against her black fur. She moved
quietly. Only the creak of the door
showed she had gone inside.

That was Slinker.
No one sees Slinker come and go.

The three cats waited in the shed. They waited silently. They sat on old sacks, thinking cat thoughts.

In one corner, in the shadows, was a cage. Slinker sniffed it.

Suddenly, the shed door banged open.

The biggest cat of all sprang into the
shed. The door crashed shut behind him.
He was the colour of marmalade except for
one strange thing.

He had one black paw.

The Big Paw had come.

Chapter 2
What's in the Cage?

The Big Paw stared at the other three.

"Hi, you guys," he said, and started to wash his black paw.

"What's happening tonight, Boss?" asked Dodger.

"Got some news," said The Big Paw. "News of a party at Number 25, in the moonlight. They're having chicken legs. The best."

All four cats licked their lips.

"Let's plan a smash and grab," said The Big Paw. "A fast one. The food's all ready to barbecue. We grab what we want and get out."

"They've got a dog," said Slinker.

"No problem," said Scrapper. He stretched out his front paws.

The claws flicked out. "I'll deal with it."

"Here's the plan," said The Big Paw.

"Scrapper, you sort the dog. Slinker and Dodger, get to the food. Grab as many chicken legs as you can carry and get back through that hole in the fence.

"Scrapper and I will pick up what we can and follow you. Just make it fast."

Then there was a surprise.

"Will there be lettuce?" said a little voice.

The cats froze.

"Will there?"

They heard a scrabbling noise. They all looked at the cage.

Two bright eyes peeped out. They saw a creature which seemed very fluffy. Its hair was long and blonde.

"Hi, Kid," said The Big Paw.

"I'm not a child. I'm a long-haired hamster," said the creature. "I'm Hattie."

The Big Paw and Scrapper growled, but Slinker said, "You don't really like lettuce, do you?"

"I love it," answered Hattie, "especially the sort you get at parties.

Red.

Green.

Frilly.

Crunchy.

I love it all. I'm coming with you."

The Big Paw smiled. "Sorry, Kid," he said. "This is a cat gang. We're mad. We're bad. We're dangerous to know. You just stay at home and fix your fur."

Hattie put her paw on the catch of her cage. Click! She was out.

"You need me to help you," she said.

The Badcats began to laugh. Scrapper laughed so much, he had to wipe his eyes on the back of his paw.

"Whiffy kippers!" snorted The Big Paw. "Don't be stupid!"

Hattie stared hard at The Big Paw. "When you came in," she said, "you banged the door shut. It's locked now."

They all looked at the shed door.

"She's right, Boss," said Dodger.

"I'll just run up the side of this deck chair, shall I?" said Hattie. "Then I can open it for you."

Chapter 3
Puddings and Burgers

The Badcats slipped out of the shed.
They padded silently down the path.
Hattie followed. A cloud covered the
moon.

"Ow!" said The Big Paw. "I've banged
my toe on that horrible garden gnome."

"Do be quiet," whispered Hattie.
"This is supposed to be a surprise smash
and grab."

"Listen, Kid," growled The Big Paw,
"I'm the Boss around here."

He glared down at Hattie. He seemed
to grow larger as his fur stood on end. He
gave a snarl and put his paw on the little
hamster. His big black paw.

"Take your paw off me or I'll squeal and squeal."

The Big Paw looked around at all the nearby houses. Someone would hear. He took his paw off the hamster.

"Whiffy kippers!" he said, crossly.

Slinker led the way to the fence.
One by one, they slipped through the hole
at the bottom. Then they stopped.

Lights hung from trees, floated in the
pond and lined the path. A very bright
light shone on some chairs and tables. A
red glow came from the barbecue.

"Look," said Dodger, "they're
getting the food ready."

The Big Paw licked his lips. There were two big tables. On one were creamy puddings and chocolate cake.

"I love cream," said Slinker.

"I can eat a whole chocolate cake," said Dodger.

"Where's the lettuce?" asked Hattie.

On the other table were fat burgers, a shiny silvery fish and a huge pile of chicken legs.

Scrapper gave a little mew. His mouth watered. "I'm going to have burgers, fish AND chicken legs," he said.

"Not so fast," growled The Big Paw. "The Boss eats first."

"Where's the lettuce?" asked Hattie.

Just then, a girl came out of the house carrying a big bowl of lettuce. A boy followed with a big bowl of fruit.

"It's my sort of party," said Hattie.

Soon, the garden was full of laughing, chatting people. One man started cooking.

A delicious smell reached the
Badcats' noses.

"Right," said The Big Paw, "Scrapper,
keep an eye on the house door. The dog
must still be inside. Dodger and Slinker,
creep under the tables. When I give the
signal 'Now!' grab what you can. I'll run
around the top of the fence and keep an eye
on things. Are you ready?"

Chapter 4
Smash and Grab

"Yes, Boss," said all the cats.

"What about me?" asked Hattie.

"Whiffy kippers," said The Big Paw.
"Stay here, Kid. Don't move. I'll try and
grab you a piece of lettuce."

Hattie sniffed. She didn't say anything.
She watched The Big Paw jump on to
the fence. She saw Scrapper slip quickly
through the legs of the guests. He was
heading for the kitchen door.

Then in the doorway, she saw
the dog.

He was a big dog.
He was very big.
He was ENORMOUS.

He was hairy. He was hungry.
He was mean. He sniffed the air.
He could smell cat!

Scrapper crouched under a chair.
He put out his claws. He lashed his tail
and he spat.

The dog saw Scrapper. They both
leaped at each other.

"Whiffy kippers!" gasped The Big Paw,
as he looked down from the fence.

Then he heard Scrapper give a terrible
yowl.

The Big Paw slipped.
He was falling.

He fell on to the table,
nose first into the
chocolate cake.

"Ow!" he yelled.
It did sound a bit like "Now!"

Dodger jumped. He was on the plate of burgers.

Slinker jumped. A woman screamed and Slinker missed the table. Slinker swung on the tablecloth. A man tried to pull her off and the cloth came, too. So did the burgers, fish and chicken legs.

The Big Paw had chocolate in his eyes and up his nose. Scrapper and the hairy dog were leaping and snarling. Everyone was shouting, running and flapping around the garden.

"Oh, for goodness sake!" said Hattie.

Hattie ran straight through everyone's legs. She tripped up the man who was trying to catch Slinker. Slinker got away with a burger.

Dodger had already taken two chicken legs through the fence.

Hattie ran straight up to the girl.

"Mummy, Mummy!" screamed the girl.
"It's the little hamster from next door.
Save the hamster."

"Be careful everyone," shouted the
mother. "It's next door's hamster."

"Shut the dog indoors," shouted
the father. "Next door's hamster is in the
garden."

Someone grabbed the hairy dog's
collar.

Scrapper streaked to the left. He picked up a chicken leg and made it to the fence.

On the other side, Slinker and Dodger had a pile of food. While everyone had been looking at Hattie, they had been back for second helpings.

But where was The Big Paw?

Chapter 5
Hattie Comes Home

The girl was holding Hattie in her arms.

"Never mind," she whispered. "Don't be frightened. I'll find you some lovely lettuce, for a treat."

The boy was holding The Big Paw. He held him very tightly.

The Big Paw wriggled and jiggled
but the boy would not let him go.

"What a mess," said the mother. "At
least we saved the hamster from those
awful cats." Then she looked at the boy.

"What are you doing? Just look at your
best shirt!" she shrieked.

The boy dropped The Big Paw. He ran straight to the fence. He was under and out in a second.

The boy was left with a print of a chocolate cat on his nice white shirt.

Back in the shed, the Badcats chewed. They were happy. They had four chicken legs, two burgers and a whole silvery fish.

"Of course," said The Big Paw, "I had to fight my way out. First, the father tried to block me. Then the boy tried to grab me. I think the mother was chasing me with the barbecue fork. Then they let the dog out again."

"You *are* brave," said Slinker.

"You have to be when you're the Boss,"
said The Big Paw. "Tell you what, you
can all lick some of the chocolate off me
for afters."

"I wonder what happened to that
hamster?" said Dodger.

"She was clever," said Scrapper.
"They all looked at her and we got
away."

"It was all in my plan," said
The Big Paw.

That wasn't true but a Badcat just
doesn't care.

In the distance, they heard voices.
Footsteps were coming down the path.

The Badcats hid under sacks.
"I think the hamster is all right."
It was the girl's voice.

"No harm done," said someone else.
"I'll put her back in her cage. The catch
must have been left undone. Thank you for
all the lovely lettuce."

The shed door opened. Someone
came in carrying a box of lettuce.
The lettuce was red, green, frilly
and crunchy.

On top of the pile was Hattie. She was
nibbling happily.

"Whiffy kippers," muttered
The Big Paw.

Although Hattie loves lettuce, other hamsters should not be fed too much of it. Lettuce can make them very poorly when eaten in large quantities.

About the author

The two cats from next door kept going into our garage. Then I saw a big cat, a stranger, was slipping in as well. Was it a meeting? Are they a gang? What were they talking about?

That's how my story started. As I wrote it, I could look out of my window and often see the cats. They just looked like ordinary cats, washing themselves in the sun, but I knew what they were planning. Now you know as well!